Children's Travel Activity Book & Journal
My Trip to Cyprus

TravelJournalBooks

CONTENTS

Hi, I hope you enjoy this book. It is jam packed with cool stuff for you to do from crosswords, word searches, drawing, coloring and quizzes. It has loads of fun things for you to do in Cyprus

Have FUN in CYPRUS

FOR YOUR PARENTS

We hope you enjoy your trip and thank you for buying our book, keep it safe as it is a great keepsake of your child's early years.

If you like this book, please leave us a review or provide feedback.

We have books for a number of holiday destinations at:

www.TravelJournalBooks.com

Bonus:
We have provided a bonus for you on page 83. We hope it helps.

This is my Journal

My Name: Nahla

Age:

Parent's name:

Tel:

Address:

Important Information

Cool Places in Cyprus for Kids

Battlefield Live Cyprus	✓
Choirokitia Village	
Tombs of the Kings	
Archaeological Museum (Nicosia)	
Kourion Archaelogical Site	
Natural History Museum (Larnaca)	
Camel Park	
Larnaka Municipal Museum of Natural History	
Limassol and Larnaca Carnival Festival	
Xyliatos Dam	
Chantara waterfall and Omodos village	
Pafos Zoo	
Santa Marina Retreat, Lemesos District	

Fig Tree Bay, Protaras	
Cyprus Motor Museum	
Limassol Castle	
Lady Mile Beach	
Sayious Adventure Park	
Aphrodite Waterpark	
Ayia Napa Water World	
Fasouri Watermania Water Park	

Do your own research to find out what other places you would like to visit

Best Websites to Research Further

Do some more research on the internet and add other cool places you find:

www.TravelJournalBooks.com/Cyprus We keep this fully updated with the best places
www.wikipedia.org/wiki/Cyprus
www.visitcyprus.com
www.theculturetrip.com/europe/cyprus
www.lonelyplanet.com/cyprus
www.chooseyourcyprus.com
www.cypnet.co.uk
www.cyprustourist.com

More cool places I want to visit on our trip

1. _____

2. _____

3. _____

4. _____

5. _____

6. _____

7. _____

8. _____

9. _____

10. _____

11. _____

12. _____

13. _____

14. _____

15. _____

Who do I want to send postcards to?

Name:
Address:

Name:
Address:

Name:
Address:

Name:
Address:

Name:

Address:

Name:

Address:

Name:

Address:

Name:

Address:

Name:

Address:

Packing List

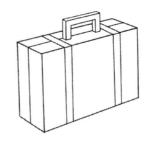

✓	This Book
	Tickets
	Passport
	Money
	Chargers
	Batteries
	Book to read
	Camera
	Tablet
	Sun glasses
	Sun cream
	Medication
	Jacket

	Toys
	Games
	Watch
	Snacks
	Umbrella
	Towel
	Guide book
	Add more below ...

Activities to do on the way to Cyprus

Cool facts, word search and other fun activities

Answers and solutions are at the back of the book

Cool Facts About Cyprus

- Cyprus is the largest island in the eastern Mediterranean but the third smallest country in the European Union

- The five main communities living in Cyprus are Greek Cypriots, Turkish Cypriots, Armenians, Latins and Maronites

- Cyprus has two official languages, Greek and Turkish

- The Cyprus Mouflon is a rare sheep that is only found in the mountain of Cyprus. It is a national symbol of Cyprus

- The Greek Roman theatre in Kourion archeological site is remarkable and has unique acoustic qualities that you can even hear the sound of a coin falling

- The patron goddess of Cyprus is Aphrodite, the Greek goddess of love. Legend has it that Aphrodite emerged from the sea in Pafos in a surge of sea foam. Hence, the place is called Petra tou Romiou (Aphrodite's Rock & Beach)

- The Capital of Cyprus is Nicosia or Lefkosia in Greek. It was named after Lefkon trees

- Cyprus was under British rule, before becoming independent in 1960

Big Cyprus Word Search

Cypriots

Lemesos

Kourion

Troodos

Commandaria

Ayia Napa

Aphrodite

Lefkosia

Nicosia

S	Q	U	E	A	H	G	N	V	G	Y	N	E	X	Z	T
U	O	F	X	A	P	J	O	V	J	D	O	B	C	F	T
F	D	S	I	Z	L	H	D	L	E	J	I	G	Y	X	U
Q	F	W	E	T	Q	V	R	M	U	E	R	K	P	L	D
R	L	R	J	M	M	W	G	O	O	K	U	Y	R	Q	R
O	E	B	G	M	E	U	I	S	D	F	O	K	I	X	T
B	V	S	F	H	M	L	O	A	V	I	K	Z	O	E	C
C	O	M	M	A	N	D	A	R	I	A	T	N	T	Q	I
M	Y	M	L	O	O	Y	X	R	Y	M	D	E	S	J	J
Y	G	L	Z	O	I	N	I	C	O	S	I	A	U	E	Y
D	Q	A	R	A	J	E	Z	U	Z	A	T	Y	G	A	H
V	L	T	N	K	O	V	G	S	P	E	D	N	E	T	L
M	W	A	I	D	P	D	T	M	W	U	V	G	S	U	B
Z	P	L	D	W	P	D	Z	V	D	H	I	P	Z	S	K
A	M	A	I	S	O	K	F	E	L	B	J	Y	V	O	R
C	G	N	C	E	L	E	U	B	V	E	V	K	W	A	E

Great Cypriot Crossword

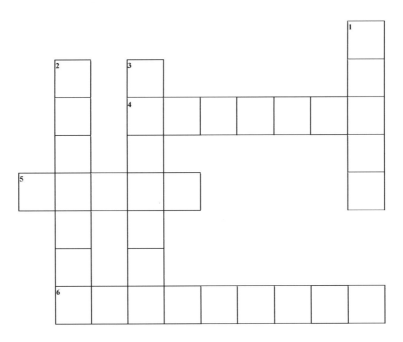

Across

4   Commandaria is said to be the oldest what in the world

5   Which part of Cyprus is Turkish-Cyprus located in?

6   The patron goddess of Cyprus

Down

1.   One of the main languages in Cyprus

2.   The capital of Cyprus is?

3.   Cyprus was under what rule, before becoming independent in 1960

Link Up Cyprus

Link the letters, to make a word or phrase

Petra tou	Castle
Limassol	Hammam
Halloumi	Castle
Kolossi	Zenobia
Aphrodite's	Romiou
Omeriye	Napa
Troodos	Mountains
Wreck of	Village
Choirokitia	Cheese
Ayia	Rock

Code Puzzle

Use the number codes to find names of popular beaches in Cyprus
(Tip 1=A, 2=B, 3=C)

14	9	19	19	9

16	9	19	19	15	21	18	9

6	9	7		20	18	5	5
			▓				

12	1	18	1		2	1	25
				▓			

3	15	18	1	12		2	1	25
					▓			

16	18	15	20	1	18	1	19

Tile Puzzle

Rearrange the tiles to reveal the answer

Clue: The patron goddess of Cyprus

TE	RO	A	DI	PH

_____

Clue: The capital of Cyprus

NI	SI	CO	A

_____

Clue: An original Cypriot cheese

MI	LO	HAL	U

_____

Clue: Principal seaport in Cyprus

PO	AS	RT	LIM	SOL

_____

Mix Up

Unscramble each of the anagram clue words; each of them is a famous place or a word related to Cyprus.

Copy the letters in the numbered cells to other cells with the same number to reveal the hidden message.

SURPYC

C	Y	P	R	U	
					7

MOONUFL

	O	U	F	L	O	N
3						

RITUSKH

	U	R	K	I	S	H
8						

AIYA APAN

	Y	I	A		N		P	A
9						2		

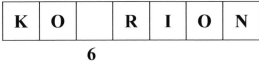

IONOURK

K	O		R	I	O	N

6

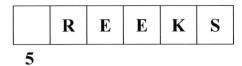

EGKSER

	R	E	E	K	S

5

AARNACL

L		R	N	A	C	A

4

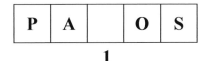

FOPAS

P	A		O	S

1

Hidden Message

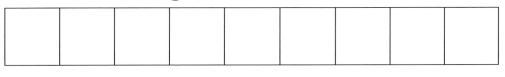

1	2	3	4	5	6	7	8	9

The Fallen Message Puzzle

Each letter appears in the correct column, but below where it should be.
You must put the letters back in the grid to rebuild the message.

	E		U		I		U	
		S		A		D		
			O					
		C		P		U		

			O	P				
		S	L	A	N	D		
	I	A	U	F	I	F	U	
B	E	C	Y	T	R	U	S	L

24

Code Cracker

1. Solve the numbers puzzle

2. Convert the answer to a letter (1=A, 2=B, 3=C).
   Crack the secret code word.

					Number			Letter
2	+	10	=			=		
14	-	13	=			=		
9	+	9	=			=		
13	-	12	=			=		
1	+	1	=			=		
3	+	2	=			=		
9	-	8	=			=		
1	+	2	=			=		
6	+	2	=			=		

Number Chains

1. Work out the math puzzle for each column below
2. Find the secret word, using the code (1=A, 2=B, 3=C)

9	4	34	52	13	10	7	44	7
+	+	-	+	-	+	-	+	-
26	12	29	12	7	11	5	44	6
=	=	=	=	=	=	=	=	=
+	-	+	-	+	-	+	-	+
43	8	1	59	6	19	15	60	16
=	=	=	=	=	=	=	=	=
-	+	+	+	+	+	-	-	-
77	8	2	13	3	2	8	8	12
=	=	=	=	=	=	=	=	=

Enter the letters above using the number code (1=A, 2=B, 3=C)

A-Mazing Maze

Can you find your way through the maze?

Color Cyprus

Color the Flag of Cyprus

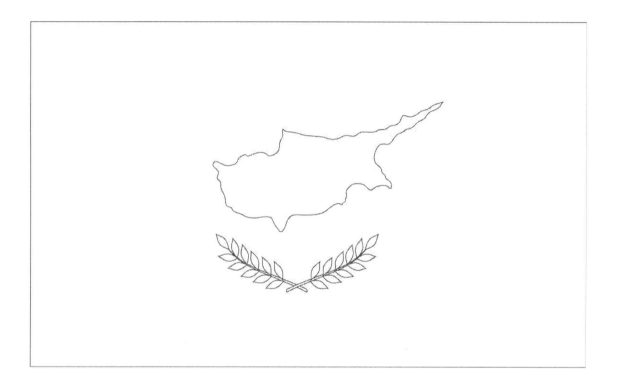

Colors: White background, Orange island, Green olive branch

Cyprus Trip Diary

Write a daily diary during your trip

Day 1   Tip! Parents see page 83

Date: _____

Weather: _____

What we did today

_____

_____

_____

_____

_____

_____

_____

Cool food of the day: _____

What I liked best today: _____

Funny thing of the day: _____

Draw something you saw today

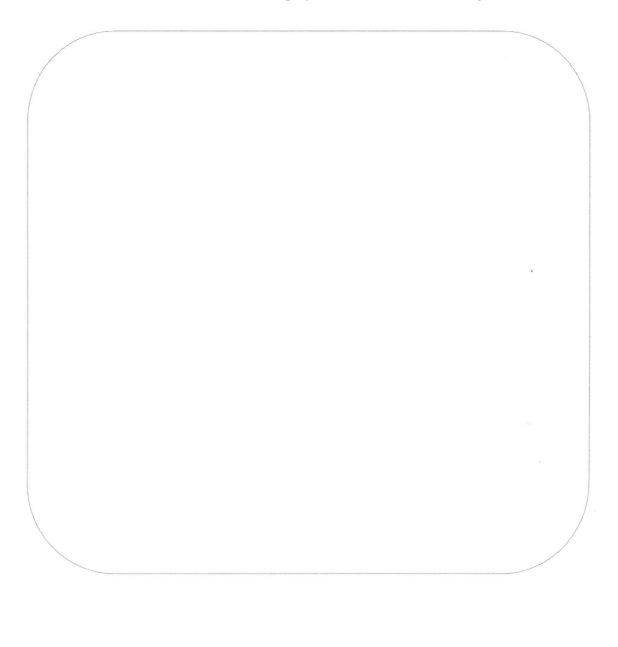

My picture is of: _____

Day 2

Date: _____

Weather: _____

What we did today

_____

_____

_____

_____

_____

_____

_____

Cool food of the day: _____

What I liked best today: _____

Funny thing of the day: _____

Draw something you saw today

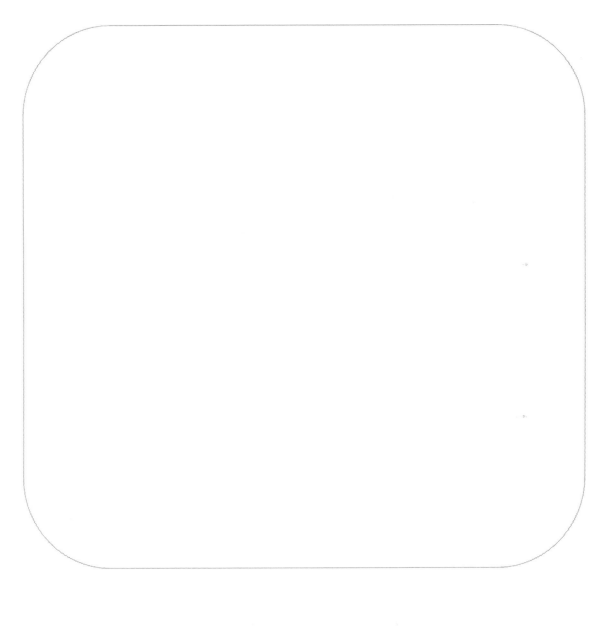

My picture is of: _____

Day 3

Date: ....

Weather: ....

What we did today

....

....

....

....

....

....

Cool food of the day: ....

What I liked best today: ....

Funny thing of the day: ....

Draw something you saw today

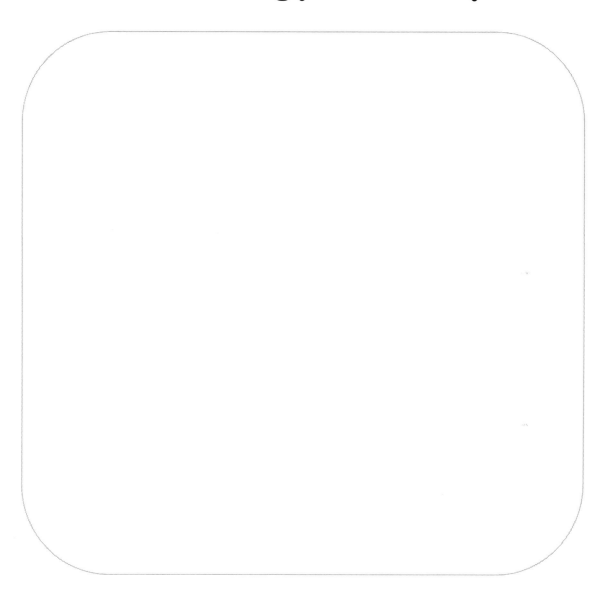

My picture is of: _____

Day 4

Date: _____

Weather: _____

What we did today

_____

_____

_____

_____

_____

_____

_____

Cool food of the day: _____

What I liked best today: _____

Funny thing of the day: _____

Draw something you saw today

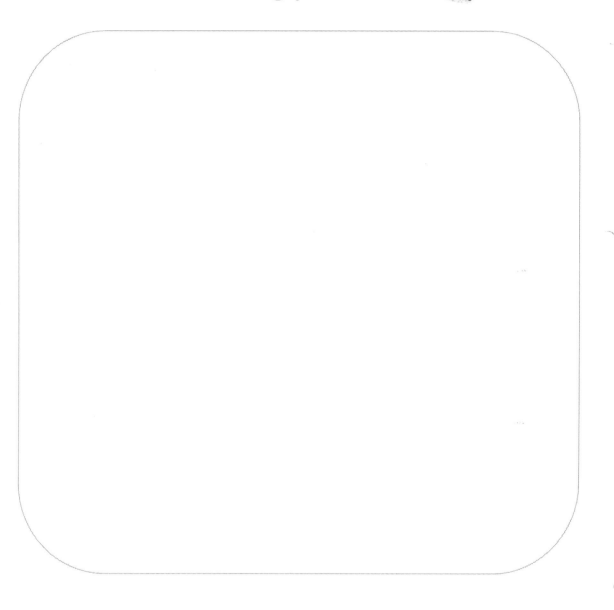

My picture is of: _____

Day 5   Tip! Send your postcards

Date: _____

Weather: _____

What we did today

_____

_____

_____

_____

_____

_____

Cool food of the day: _____

What I liked best today: _____

Funny thing of the day: _____

Draw something you saw today

My picture is of: _____

Day 6

Date: _____

Weather: _____

What we did today

_____

_____

_____

_____

_____

_____

Cool food of the day: _____

What I liked best today: _____

Funny thing of the day: _____

Draw something you saw today

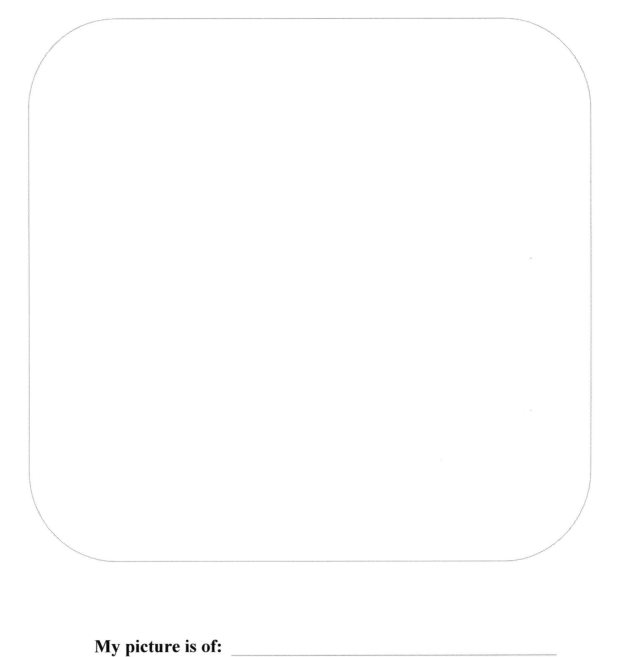

My picture is of: _____

Day 7

Date: _____

Weather: _____

What we did today

_____

_____

_____

_____

_____

_____

Cool food of the day: _____

What I liked best today: _____

Funny thing of the day: _____

Draw something you saw today

My picture is of: Me and daddy on a paraglider

Day 8

Date: _____

Weather: _____

What we did today

_____

_____

_____

_____

_____

_____

Cool food of the day: _____

What I liked best today: _____

Funny thing of the day: _____

Draw something you saw today

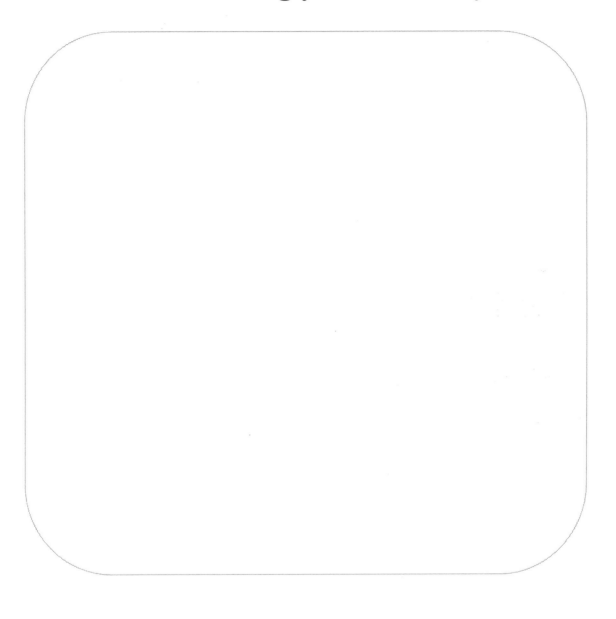

My picture is of: _____

Day 9

Date: _____

Weather: _____

What we did today

_____

_____

_____

_____

_____

Cool food of the day: _____

What I liked best today: _____

Funny thing of the day: _____

Draw something you saw today

My picture is of: _____

Day 10

Date: _____

Weather: _____

What we did today

_____

_____

_____

_____

_____

_____

_____

Cool food of the day: _____

What I liked best today: _____

Funny thing of the day: _____

Draw something you saw today

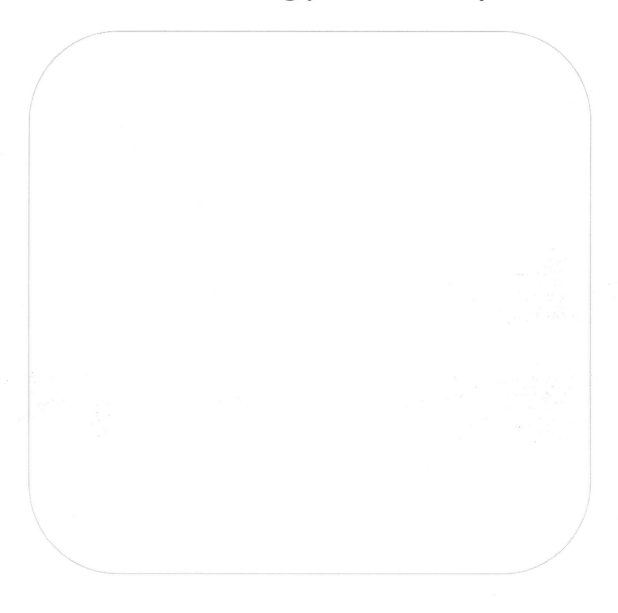

My picture is of: _____

Day 11

Date:

Weather:

What we did today

_____

_____

_____

_____

_____

_____

_____

Cool food of the day:

What I liked best today:

Funny thing of the day:

Draw something you saw today

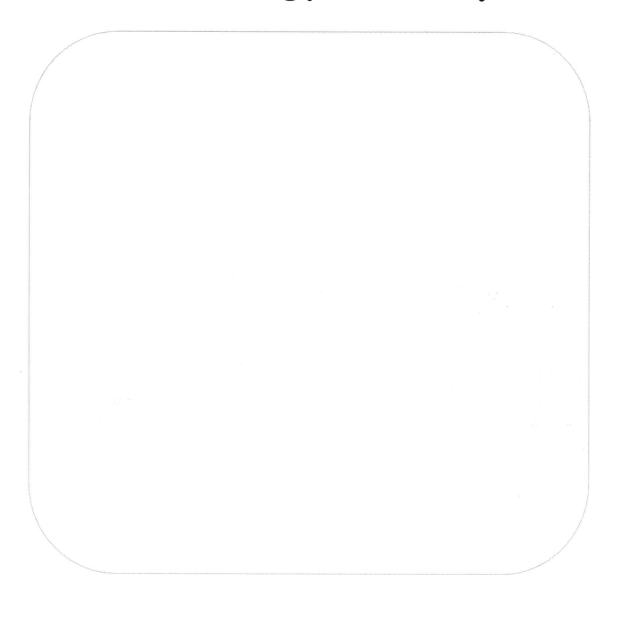

My picture is of: _____

Day 12

Date: _____

Weather: _____

What we did today

_____

_____

_____

_____

_____

_____

_____

Cool food of the day: _____

What I liked best today: _____

Funny thing of the day: _____

Draw something you saw today

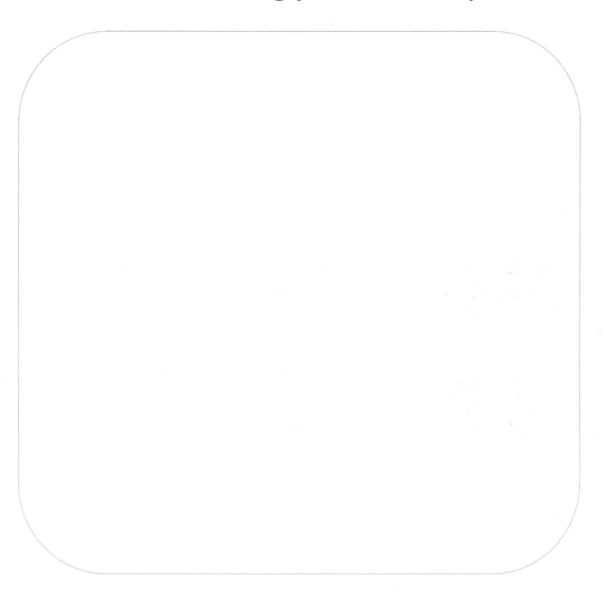

My picture is of: _____

Day 13

Date: _____

Weather: _____

What we did today

_____

_____

_____

_____

_____

_____

_____

Cool food of the day: _____

What I liked best today: _____

Funny thing of the day: _____

Draw something you saw today

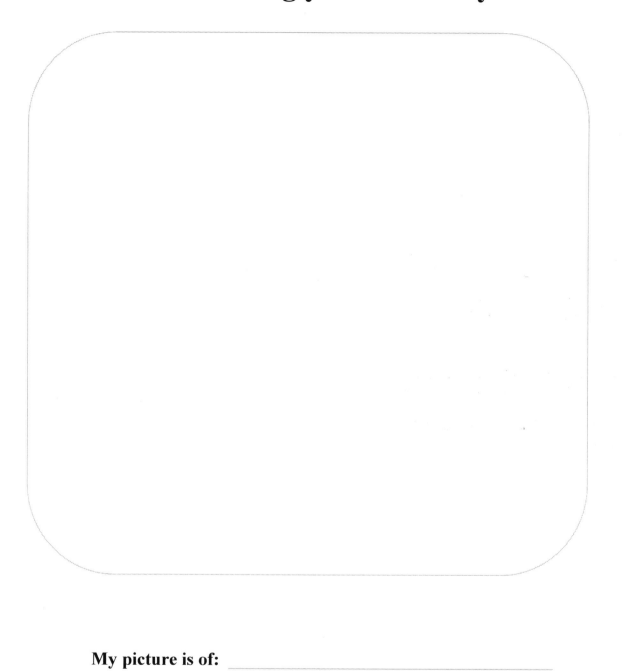

My picture is of: _____

Day 14

Date: _____

Weather: _____

What we did today

_____

_____

_____

_____

_____

_____

Cool food of the day: _____

What I liked best today: _____

Funny thing of the day: _____

Draw something you saw today

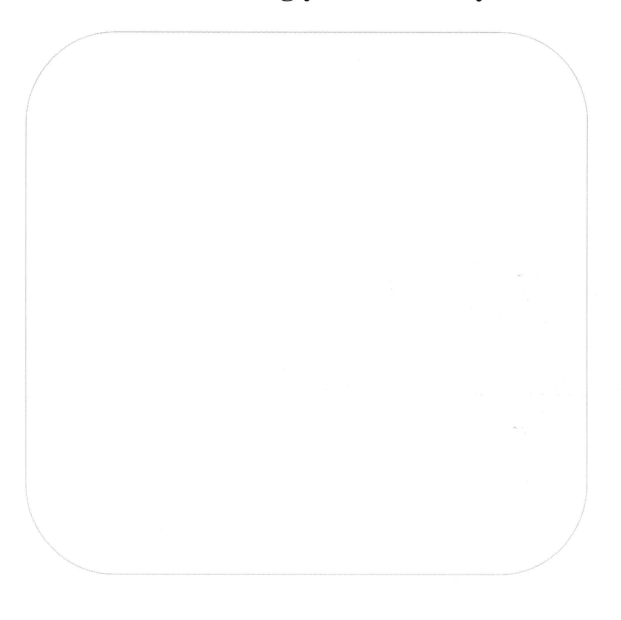

My picture is of: _____

Activities for the Trip Home

Quiz, drawing and coloring fun, for your trip home

Answers and solutions are at the back of the book

Big Cyprus Quiz

(Circle the correct answer)

1. What is the capital of Cyprus?

    Paphos   Limassol

    Nicosia   Protaras

2. What is the largest ethnic group in Cyprus?

    Armenians   Greeks

    Maronites   Turkish

3. In what year did Cyprus become part of the European Union?

    2003   1999

    2004   2008

4. What is the name of the place dividing the Greek-Cyprus from the Turkish-Cyprus?

    Red Line   Green Line

    Green Mile   Morphou

5. The population of Cyprus is estimated to be

   10 million   1.1 million

   5.3 million   3.2 million

6. Who is the patron goddess of Cyprus?

   Hera   Aphrodite

   Athena   Ceres

7. 'Cyprus' is derived from the Latin word *cuprum* which means

   Cypress   Gold

   Copper   Bronze

8. What is the literal meaning of Petra tou Romiou?

   Peter's Rock   Rock of the Greek

   Greek Stone   Aphrodite's rock

9. What is the second largest city in Cyprus and is considered the center of the wine-making industry?

   Famagusta   Larnaca

   Limassol   Pafos

10. What is the highest point in Cyprus measuring 1951 meters above sea level?

       Troodos Mountain   Mesaoria

       Mount Olympus   Kyrenia Range

11. This town in Cyprus is the birthplace of the philosopher Zeno and second home of Saint Lazarus

       Larnaka   Lefkosia

       Pafos   Famagusta

12. Popular cheese in Cyprus

       Stilton   Halloumi

       Fromage   Chedder

13. The oldest red wine in the world

       Vert   Commandaria

       Vino   Rouge

Draw Cyprus

Draw some of the cool things you saw in Cyprus, during your trip

72

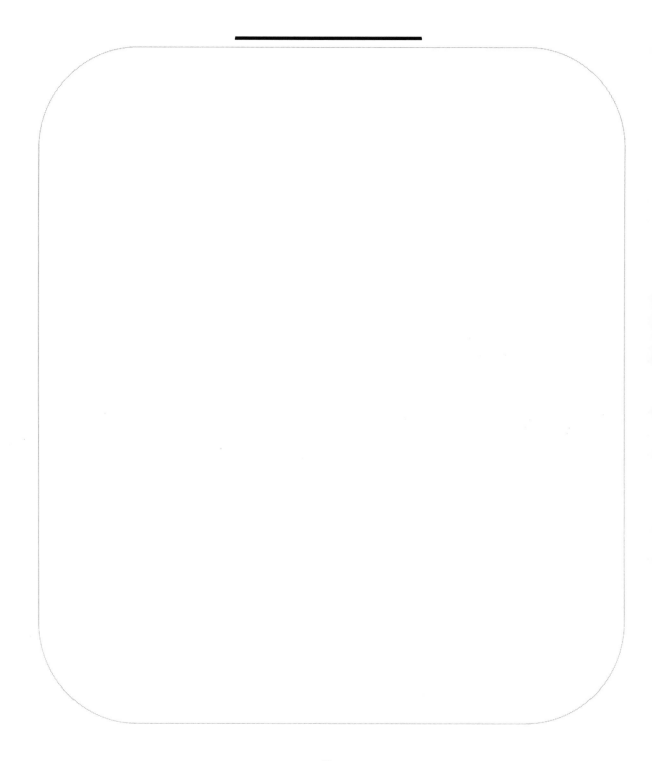

Color the Flag of Cyprus

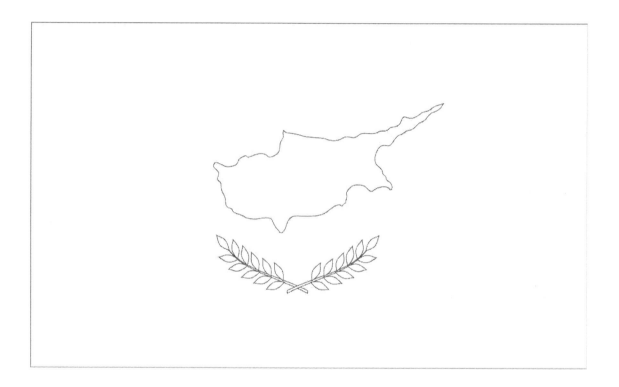

Colors: White background, Orange island, Green olive branch

Things I will remember from our trip

Favorite Places we visited on our Trip

We hope you enjoyed your trip to Cyprus

Don't forget to thank Mom and Dad

Useful Resources for Mom & Dad

Children's Shoe Sizes

UK	EUROPE	US	Japan
4	20	4½ or 5	12 ½
4 ½	21	5 or 5½	13
5	21 or 22	5½ or 6	13 ½
5 ½	22	6	13½ or 14
6	23	6½ or 7	14 or 14½
6 ½	23 or 24	7 ½	14½ or 15
7	24	7½ or 8	15
7 ½	25	8 or 9	15 ½
8	25 or 26	8½ or 9	16
8 ½	26	9½	16 ½
9	27	9½ or 10	16 ½ or 17
10	28	10½ or 11	17 ½
10½ or 11	29	11½ or 12	18
11 ½	30	12½	18 or 18 ½
12	31	13	19 or 19 ½
12 ½	31	13 or 13½	19 ½ or 20
13	32	1	20
13 ½	32 ½	1 ½	20 ½
1	33	1½ or 2	21
2	34	2½ or 3	22

Children's Clothing Sizes

UK	EUROPE	US	Australia
12m	80cm	12-18m	12m
18m	80-86cm	18-24m	18m
24m	86-92cm	23-24m	2
2-3	92-98cm	2T	3
3-4	98-104cm	4T	4
3-5	104-110cm	5	5
5-6	110-116cm	6	6
6-7	116-122cm	6X-7	7
7-8	122-128cm	7 to 8	8
8-9	128-134cm	9 to 10	9
9-10	134-140cm	10	10
10-11	140-146cm	11	11
11-12	146-152cm	14	12

Women's Shoe Sizes

UK	EUROPE	US	Japan
3	35 ½	5	22 ½
3 ½	36	5 ½	23
4	37	6	23
4 ½	37 ½	6 ½	23 ½
5	38	7	24
5 ½	39	7 ½	24
6	39 ½	8	24 ½
6 ½	40	8 ½	25
7	41	9 ½	25 ½
7 ½	41 ½	10	26
8	42	10 ½	26 ½

Women's Clothes Sizes

UK	US	Japan	France / Spain	Germany	Italy	Australia
6/8	6	7-9	36	34	40	8
10	8	9-11	38	36	42	10
12	10	11-13	40	38	44	12
14	12	13-15	42	39	46	14
16	14	15-17	44	40	48	16
18	16	17-19	46	42	50	18
20	18	19-21	48	44	52	20

Men's Shoe Sizes

UK	EUROPE	US	Japan
6	38 ½	6 ½	24 ½
6 ½	39	7	25
7	40	7 ½	25 ½
7 ½	41	8	26
8	42	8 ½	27 ½
8 ½	43	9	27 ½
9	43 ½	9 ½	28
9 ½	44	10	28 ½
10	44	10 ½	28 ½
10 ½	44 ½	11	29
11	45	12	29 ½

Men's Suit / Coat / Sweater Sizes

UK / US / Aus	EU / Japan	General
32	42	Small
34	44	Small
36	46	Small
38	48	Medium
40	50	Large
42	52	Large
44	54	Extra Large
46	56	Extra Large

Men's Pants / Trouser Sizes (Waist)

UK / US	Europe
32	81 cm
34	86 cm
36	91 cm
38	97 cm
40	102 cm
42	107 cm

Puzzles Answers and Solutions

Big Cyprus Word Search

Cypriots

Lemesos

Kourion

Troodos

Commandaria

Ayia Napa

Aphrodite

Lefkosia

Nicosia

S	Q	U	E	A	H	G	N	V	G	Y	N	E	X	Z	T
U	O	F	X	A	P	J	O	V	J	D	O	B	C	F	T
F	D	S	I	Z	L	H	D	L	E	J	I	G	Y	X	U
Q	F	W	E	T	Q	V	R	M	U	E	R	K	P	L	D
R	L	R	J	M	M	W	G	O	O	K	U	Y	R	Q	R
O	E	B	G	M	E	U	I	S	D	F	O	K	I	X	T
B	V	S	F	H	M	L	O	A	V	I	K	Z	O	E	C
C	O	M	M	A	N	D	A	R	I	A	T	N	T	Q	I
M	Y	M	L	O	O	Y	X	R	Y	M	D	E	S	J	J
Y	G	L	Z	O	I	N	I	C	O	S	I	A	U	E	Y
D	Q	A	R	A	J	E	Z	U	Z	A	T	Y	G	A	H
V	L	T	N	K	O	V	G	S	P	E	D	N	E	T	L
M	W	A	I	D	P	D	T	M	W	U	V	G	S	U	B
Z	P	L	D	W	P	D	Z	V	D	H	I	P	Z	S	K
A	M	A	I	S	O	K	F	E	L	B	J	Y	V	O	R
C	G	N	C	E	L	E	U	B	V	E	V	K	W	A	E

Great Cypriot Crossword

								G
N		B						R
I		R	E	D	W	I	N	E
C		I						E
N	O	R	T	H				K
S		T						
I		I						
A	P	H	R	O	D	I	T	E

Across

4   Commandaria is said to be the oldest what in the world

5   Which part of Cyprus is Turkish-Cyprus located in?

6   The patron goddess of Cyprus

Down

1.   One of the main languages in Cyprus

2.   The capital of Cyprus is?

3.   Cyprus was under what rule, before becoming independent in 1960

Link Up Cyprus

Link the letters, to make a word or phrase

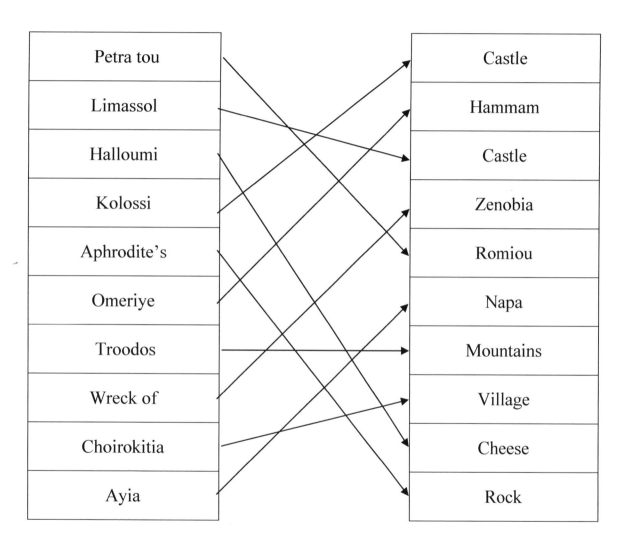

Petra tou	Castle
Limassol	Hammam
Halloumi	Castle
Kolossi	Zenobia
Aphrodite's	Romiou
Omeriye	Napa
Troodos	Mountains
Wreck of	Village
Choirokitia	Cheese
Ayia	Rock

Code Puzzle

Use the number codes to find names of popular beaches in Cyprus

(Tip 1=A, 2=B, 3=C)

14	9	19	19	9
N	I	S	S	I

16	9	19	19	15	21	18	9
P	I	S	S	O	U	R	I

6	9	7		20	18	5	5
F	I	G		T	R	E	E

12	1	18	1		2	1	25
L	A	R	A		B	A	Y

3	15	18	1	12		2	1	25
C	O	R	A	L		B	A	Y

16	18	15	20	1	18	1	19
P	R	O	T	A	R	A	S

Tile Puzzle

Rearrange the tiles to reveal the answer

Clue: The patron goddess of Cyprus

TE	RO	A	DI	PH

APHRODITE

Clue: The capital of Cyprus

NI	SI	CO	A

NICOSIA

Clue: An original Cypriot cheese

MI	LO	HAL	U

HALLOUMI

Clue: Principal seaport in Cyprus

PO	AS	RT	LIM	SOL

LIMASSOL PORT

Mix Up

Unscramble each of the anagram clue words; each of them is a famous place or a word related to Cyprus.

Copy the letters in the numbered cells to other cells with the same number to reveal the hidden message.

SURPYC

C	Y	P	R	U	S
					7

MOONUFL

M	O	U	F	L	O	N
3						

RITUSKH

T	U	R	K	I	S	H
8						

AIYA APAN

A	Y	I	A		N	A	P	A
9						2		

IONOURK

K	O	U	R	I	O	N

6

EGKSER

G	R	E	E	K	S

5

AARNACL

L	A	R	N	A	C	A

4

FOPAS

P	A	F	O	S

1

Hidden Message

F	A	M	A	G	U	S	T	A
1	2	3	4	5	6	7	8	9

The Fallen Message Puzzle

Each letter appears in the correct column, but below where it should be.
You must put the letters back in the grid to rebuild the message.

B	E	A	U	T	I	F	U	L
	I	S	L	A	N	D		
			O	F				
		C	Y	P	R	U	S	

				O	P			
		S	L	A	N	D		
	I	A	U	F	I	F	U	
B	E	C	Y	T	R	U	S	L

Code Cracker

1. Solve the numbers puzzle

2. Convert the answer to a letter (1=A, 2=B, 3=C).
   Crack the secret code word.

				Number		Letter
2	+	10	=	12	=	L
14	-	13	=	1	=	A
9	+	9	=	18	=	R
13	-	12	=	1	=	A
1	+	1	=	2	=	B
3	+	2	=	5	=	E
9	-	8	=	1	=	A
1	+	2	=	3	=	C
6	+	2	=	8	=	H

Number Chains

1. Work out the math puzzle for each column below
2. Find the secret word, using the code (1=A, 2=B, 3=C)

9	4	34	52	13	10	7	44	7
+	+	-	+	-	+	-	+	-
26	12	29	12	7	11	5	44	6
=	=	=	=	=	=	=	=	=
35	**16**	**5**	**64**	**6**	**21**	**2**	**88**	**1**
+	-	+	-	+	-	+	-	+
43	8	1	59	6	19	15	60	16
=	=	=	=	=	=	=	=	=
78	**8**	**6**	**5**	**12**	**2**	**17**	**28**	**17**
-	+	+	+	+	+	-	-	-
77	8	2	13	3	2	8	8	12
=	=	=	=	=	=	=	=	=
1	**16**	**8**	**18**	**15**	**4**	**9**	**20**	**5**

A	P	H	R	O	D	I	T	E

Enter the letters above using the number code (1=A, 2=B, 3=C)

Big Cyprus Quiz

(Circle the correct answer)

1. What is the capital of Cyprus?

   Paphos   Limassol

   <u>Nicosia</u>   Protaras

2. What is the largest ethnic group in Cyprus?

   Armenians   **<u>Greeks</u>**

   Maronites   Turkish

3. In what year did Cyprus become part of the European Union?

   2003   1999

   <u>2004</u>   2008

4. What is the name of the place dividing the Greek-Cyprus from the Turkish-Cyprus?

   Red Line   **<u>Green Line</u>**

   Green Mile   Morphou

5. The population of Cyprus is estimated to be

10 million	**1.1 million**
5.3 million	3.2 million

6. Who is the patron goddess of Cyprus?

Hera	**Aphrodite**
Athena	Ceres

7. 'Cyprus' is derived from the Latin word *cuprum* which means

Cypress	Gold
Copper	Bronze

8. What is the literal meaning of Petra tou Romiou?

Peter's Rock	**Rock of the Greek**
Greek Stone	Aphrodite's rock

9. What is the second largest city in Cyprus and is considered the center of the wine-making industry?

Famagusta	Larnaca
Limassol	Pafos

10. What is the highest point in Cyprus measuring 1951 meters above sea level?

Troodos Mountain   Mesaoria

Mount Olympus   Kyrenia Range

11. This town in Cyprus is the birthplace of the philosopher Zeno and second home of Saint Lazarus

Larnaka   Lefkosia

Pafos   Famagusta

12. Popular cheese in Cyprus

Stilton   **Halloumi**

Fromage   Chedder

13. The oldest red wine in the world

Vert   **Commandaria**

Vino   Rouge